CIEL PUBLISHING

THANKSGIVING
JOKES FOR KIDS

WHY DID THE TURKEY
CROSS THE ROAD?

Happy Thanksgiving!

No turkey this year?

I suspect fowl play!

TABLE OF CONTENTS

INTRODUCTION

Happy Thanksgiving!

The book you're holding was written with the goal of bringing joy and laughter to kids and grownups while celebrating one of America's favorite holidays. Thanksgiving is all about getting the family together, and so is the purpose of this book.

While these jokes can be appreciated by any single member of the family, it has been proven that each joke is 98% funnier if read out loud by one person to a room full of family members or friends who are either laughing at the jokes or groaning at the puns.

You can read while you're waiting for the meal to be cooked. You can read it on the table—be careful not to pour food on the pages. You can read it after dinner, when everybody is on the couch trying to digest the mountain of deliciousness they just had. What matters is that you do it with the people who mean the most to you.

And yes, this book does include both dad jokes and jokes that can be appreciated by non-dads. If you're not a dad, some—but not all—of these jokes will probably make you groan in pain a little bit. Think of it as a bonding experience: You will always remember that year when Dad read that really terrible turkey-related knock-knock joke that made everybody in the room look forward to Christmas.

THANKSGIVING JOKES

How would a turkey egg introduce this chapter?

These are the yolks, folks.

JOKES ABOUT TURKEYS

How can you tell a turkey has poor table manners?

They gobble their food!

What did the turkey give thanks for on Thanksgiving?

Vegans.

Are turkeys ever thankful to people in general?

They sure are... the Friday after Thanksgiving.

How many turkeys do you need to change a lightbulb?

Three: One to hold the ladder, one to screw in the light bulb, and one to remind the others that they don't have fingers and really shouldn't be doing this.

Can you guess the best time to eat a turkey?

When it's cooked and on the table.

What happens when a turkey lays an egg on the roof?

You get an eggroll.

But why do turkeys gobble?

... Because they can't talk!

How do you keep a turkey in suspenseful anticipation?

I'll tell you tomorrow.

Dad is cooking Thanksgiving dinner in the kitchen.

Mom comes in and says, "My brothers called. It turns out they're all bringing their spouses. We're going to need more food."

Dad sighed, since he was already exhausted from the cooking, and said, "Ugh! Kill me."

The turkey rolled his eyes and said, "Tell me about it."

How do you make a turkey float?

With three scoops of ice cream, root beer, and a turkey.

How long should you let the turkey rest after you take it out of the oven?

It depends on how tired it is.

Question for the magicians: How do you make a turkey disappear?

Invite your family over for Thanksgiving.

Question for the biologists: Which side of the turkey has the biggest amount of feathers?

The outside.

"My two favorite holidays are Thanksgiving and Halloween."

"Why? Just because they're close to each other? They have nothing in common."

"Of course, they do. Halloween has goblins. Thanksgiving has gobblers."

"Mom, how can you tell the difference between a chicken and a turkey?"

"Chickens celebrate Thanksgiving."

What do you call a turkey with stuffing in its ears?

Whatever you want. It can't hear you.

But what happens if we can't get a turkey for Thanksgiving?

Don't worry. We invited Uncle Jerry.

Where can you find turkeys with no legs?

Wherever you left them.

What does a teddy bear have in common with a turkey?

Both of them have stuffing inside.

"How do you know if a turkey likes you?"

"Its face turns red."

"Is your band playing a gig tonight?"

"We can't. Not on Thanksgiving."

"Why not?"

"People ate all the drumsticks!"

"How do you know if you like the turkey?"

"Your mom cooked it."

"Tommy, it's rude to stare at the turkey dressing."

"Why?"

"Because it deserves some privacy!"

Why do turkeys lay eggs?

Well, if they dropped them, they would break.

What is the technical term for the feathers on the tip of a turkey's tail?

Turkey feathers. Same as the feathers on the rest of its body!

Why did your Thanksgiving dinner put on a nice suit?

Someone told him that well-dressed turkeys had a career in politics.

What does a turkey use to get itself clean?

A feather duster.

JOKES ABOUT PILGRIMS

Why did the Pilgrims really choose the turkey to eat on Thanksgiving?

They couldn't fit a buffalo in the oven.

What do you call the number of years a Pilgrim has been alive?

His pilgrim-age.

Little known fact:

The Pilgrims actually arrived in America in April. That's because April showers bring Mayflowers.

What did the Pilgrim get at the beach?

A Puri-tan.

(Kids: Puritanism was the Pilgrim's religion, so they were called Puritans.)

What do you call the rules of the Pilgrims' language?

Pil-grammar.

The Pilgrims traveled on their ship, the Mayflower. What do college students travel on?

Scholarships!

Why did Pilgrims put buckles on their hats?

Their heads were too thin, and the hats kept falling off!

If the Pilgrims were still alive today, what would they be most well-known for?

Probably for how old they would be!

Pilgrim: "Jebediah, why are you eating that candle?"

Other Pilgrim: "I just wanted a light snack."

What kind of music did the Pilgrims rock out to?

Plymouth Rock, of course.

That's my friend over there. He's a Pilgrim. He's feeling a little down today.

He's my pal-grim.

What kind of car do Pilgrims drive?

A Plymouth.

CATCHING THE TURKEY

When is the only time turkey soup is not good for your health?

When you are the turkey.

Why are turkeys jealous of clocks, especially before Thanksgiving?

Because time flies.

Mr. Spock: "Live long and prosper."

Turkey: "I wouldn't count on it."

What is a turkey's favorite holiday?

Christmas. It means he made it.

What do you call a turkey running for its life?

Fast food.

What is the fastest way to catch a turkey?

Having a good pitcher!

"Why do we eat turkey at Thanksgiving, anyway?"

"On the very first Thanksgiving, the Pilgrims and the Natives assembled all the animals. They asked for volunteers to become the Thanksgiving meal. None of the animals stepped up, but a turkey's tail looks a lot like a hand up."

What does a turkey say to the hunter before Thanksgiving?

"Quack! Quack!"

Why did the turkey cross the road?

To go after the chicken.

Why did the turkey cross the road again?

To prove to everybody that he wasn't chicken.

What do turkeys wish for?

For people to eat duck on Thanksgiving.

Can turkeys jump higher than the Eiffel Tower?

Of course they can. Towers can't jump!

Breaking news:
Scientists have created a new breed of turkey with six legs to have enough drumsticks for a whole family at Thanksgiving.

Unfortunately, the turkeys ran away, and nobody's been able to catch them.

When a turkey has a project, what is its deadline?

The fourth Thursday of November.

What do you call a turkey that has been relaxing in the bathtub with essential oils all night?

Well marinated.

What has webbed feet and tail feathers?

A turkey wearing diving gear.

(You were thinking of a duck, weren't you?)

JOKES ABOUT FOOD

How many cranberries can grow on a bush?

All of them.
All of them grow on bushes.

What is the best thing to put on pumpkin pies?

Your teeth!

How long does a mathematician take to eat one slice of pumpkin pi?

Exactly 3.14 seconds.

Why does nobody like making bread?

It's a pretty crummy job.

Why did the pie need to go to the dentist?

It needed a filling.

TURKEY PUNS

What did they name the turkey that was really hard to see?

The Murky Turkey.

What is the key to my heart?

Today... a tur-key.

What do turkeys love having for dessert?

Apple gobblers!

"Hey, I offered that turkey some apple gobbler, but he turned it down."

"It was probably stuffed."

What did they name the weirdest turkey in the world?

The Quirky Turkey.

"Did you hear about that little turkey that got his stuffing knocked out of him by that big turkey?"

"That big turkey should have pecked on someone his own size."

What did they name the most unfriendly turkey in the world?

The Jerky Turkey.

What happens when turkeys get in a fight?

They usually get the stuffing knocked out of them.

What did they name the turkey with the nicest smile?

The Smirky Turkey.

What did they name the turkey that fell in love with a pig?

The Porky Turkey.

What did they name the place where turkeys go dancing?

The Butterball.

And what do they dance in there?

The turkey trot!

What do you call standing up late, sleeping in, eating a lot, and hanging out with gobblers?

They're the perkies of being a turkey.

Why do we like covering the turkey with fat or gravy when we're cooking it?

Probably because it appeals to our baster instincts.

What does a turkey's ringtone sound like?

"Wing-wing! Wing-wing!"

"Dude, who's the new drummer you hired for the band?"

"That's Tom."

"... Is he a turkey?"

"Yeah."

"Why did you get a turkey to be our drummer?"

"He came with his own drumsticks!"

"Hey, did you see those turkeys dancing in the parade?"

"I did. They looked like they were marching to the beat of their own drumsticks."

"Dude, you invited a turkey over for Thanksgiving, and it actually came?"

"Yup. He just made... a gravy mistake."

What do turkeys use to cross the country?

A gravy train.

What do turkeys use for sailing across the sea?

A gravy boat.

What does a turkey using the internet sound like?

"Google, Google."

What does a turkey in space sound like?

"Hubble, Hubble."

(Kids: Hubble is the name of a famous telescope that NASA sent to space in 1990.)

ABSOLUTELY FOWL PUNS

**What happens when the turkey
is undercooked?**

It puts everyone in a fowl mood.

What do turkeys think of Thanksgiving dinner tables?

They think they're a fowl sight.

What do turkeys suggest you eat at Thanksgiving instead?

Any food that doesn't taste fowl.

Why was the turkey expelled from the basketball game?

It committed a fowl.

Why was the turkey expelled from the football game?

It did a fowl play.

Why did the police arrest that turkey?

They suspected fowl play.

Why did the turkey stop playing baseball?

It kept hitting fowl balls.

Why aren't turkeys allowed to talk to children?

They use fowl language.

Why does nobody invite turkeys to their parties?

They keep making party fowls.

What kind of weather are you having if turkeys start falling from the sky?

Fowl weather.

FOOD-BASED PUNS
TURKEY NOT INCLUDED

What do you get when you accidentally sit on some sweet potatoes?

Squash casserole!

"Hey bro, what vegetables are we having with the turkey?"

"Beets me."

"Oh man, I just stepped on a grape."

"Is it okay?"

"Yeah, it just let out a little wine."

What side dish do ninjas love most?

Masked potatoes.

You shouldn't let the side dishes tell jokes during dinner. They're too corny.

What do scarecrows love to eat?

Straw-berries.

"Those beans look a little jealous of the other vegetables."

"Why do you say that?"

"They look so green!"

What is the sport pumpkins love to play?

Squash!

"I paid so much for this Thanksgiving soup."

"What, why?"

"It has twenty-four carrots."

Sweet Potato: "Hey. I think we're going to be a side dish."

Potato: "Are you sure?"

Sweet Potato: "Yes, I yam."

"The turkey seasoning tastes a little weird."

"Sorry, I ran out of thyme."

"That butter hasn't stopped making jokes all evening."

"Yeah, it really is on a roll."

What does Dracula have for Thanksgiving?

Monster Mashed potatoes and grave-y.

(Just kidding. He can only have blood.)

What is the most important role to play in any Thanksgiving meal?

The casserole.

TERIBLE, TERIBLE PUNS

What do you call a Thanksgiving meal with a rubber turkey?

Pranksgiving.

What do you call Thanksgiving if you're a vampire?

Fangsgiving.

What do you call Thanksgiving with selfish people?

Thankstaking.

What do they call Thanksgiving in the military?

Tanksgiving.

What do they call Thanksgiving at the hairdresser's?

Bangsgiving.

What do they call Thanksgiving in Canada?

Thanksgiving, eh?

What do they call Thanksgiving in Spain?

El Thanksgiving.

What does the actor who voices Woody from Toy Story call Thanksgiving?

Tom Hanksgiving.

What do you call putting gas in your car on the fourth Thursday of November?

Tanksfilling.

What do they call Thanksgiving on Wall Street?

Banksgiving.

OTHER JOKES

What is the thing that always comes at the end of Thanksgiving?

The letter G.

If you took Thanksgiving off the calendar, what would you get?

You would get a weird week with only six days.

Why do some kids arrive late to school on the day after Thanksgiving?

Because it's Black Friday, so they give the day fifty percent off.

(Don't really do that, kids.)

Why do kids' grades get so low after Thanksgiving?

Because everything is marked down after a holiday!

Ironically, what is a country that does not celebrate Thanksgiving?

Turkey.

When grown-ups are talking politics and kids are filling up their plate, what are they both doing?

They're both choosing sides.

What should you bring to Thanksgiving dinner to make it extra basic?

Pumpkin spice.

(Kids: Have your parents explain this one.)

What should you not wear to Thanksgiving dinner?

Tight pants and white shirts.

"What is Thanksgiving even for, anyway?"

"To remind us it's time to start preparing for Christmas!"

What is the thing that smells the best at Thanksgiving dinner?

Your nose, of course.

How is Thanksgiving Day like the US senate?

They're both full of turkeys.

Why did they give the Nobel Prize to the pumpkin farmer?

He was out standing in his field.

What should you get when you've eaten too much turkey and vegetables?

Dessert!

What do you call it when your family members play cards while waiting for dinner?

The Hunger Games.

In what part of the world does Christmas come before Thanksgiving?

In a dictionary.

Why does conversation always get heated up during Thanksgiving dinner?

To keep the food from going cold.

ONE-LINER JOKES

Grown-ups, feel free to use these as captions on Instagram.

THE BEST
ONE-LINERS

I thought about no longer celebrating Thanksgiving... but I can't just quit cold turkey.

Good food is what I'm craving, the turkey is what I'm carving.

You can't spell grateful without great and full!... Wait.

First the riches, then the dishes.

This is it, boys—every man for yamself.

Cheer up—you're looking pretty pil-grim.

If it all becomes too much, remember: You could be eating in your school's cafeteria right now!

I couldn't possibly eat another bite. You got any pie?

Who needs abs when you can have pumpkin pie?

Keep calm and cranberry on.

May your glasses be full, your bellies fuller, and your shirts unstained.

For first-timers, remember: The turkey needs to be dead before you cook it.

Turkey usually tastes better the day after Thanksgiving. My mom's turkey tastes better the day before she cooks it.

Most days, the President of the United States has an important job that he needs to do. And then, some days, he just has to pardon a turkey.

And if the conversation gets too heated, remember that very soon, everyone will be too stuffed to talk.

KNOCK-KNOCK JOKES

Don't say we didn't warn you.

"Knock, knock!"

"Who's there?"

"Arthur!"

"Arthur who?"

"Arthur any mashed potatoes?"

"Knock, knock!"

"Who's there?"

"Dewey."

"Dewey who?"

"Dewey have any gravy?"

"Knock, knock!"

"Who's there?"

"Annie."

"Annie who?"

"Annie body wants more pie?"

"Knock, knock!"

"Who's there?"

"A herd."

"A herd of what?"

"A herd you were having Thanksgiving dinner, so I popped by."

"Knock, knock!"

"Who's there?"

"Anita."

"Anita who?"

"Anita 'nother plate, please."

"Knock, knock!"

"Who's there?"

"Dishes."

"Dishes who?"

"Dishes a pretty bad joke."

"Knock, knock!"

"Who's there?"

"More guests for Thanksgiving!"

"Oh, dear God."

SHORT FUNNY STORIES

Here are some short stories with gags to whet your appetite before dinner.

FAVORITE PART

It was little Nathan's seventh Thanksgiving. The whole family was gathered around the table. Nate's mom watched him fidgeting with his piece of turkey.

"Hey, Nate," she said, "what is your favorite part of the turkey?"

Nate thought for a little bit. "I don't know," he said. "You give me the same part every year."

Mom slapped her forehead as the rest of the family chuckled. He was right. Soon, his parents, his siblings, and all his uncles, aunts, and cousins were giving Nate bits of turkey from their plates so he could try them—breast, wings, and drumsticks, Nate tried them all.

Afterward, Mom asked again, "So, after all that, what was your favorite bit?"

Nate shrugged. "I dunno. It all just tastes like turkey."

The family laughed. Mom rolled her eyes.

A MOMENT OF CONTEMPLATION

It was the slow, lazy hours of the afternoon after Thanksgiving dinner. Susan went outside to the porch, where her grandfather was sitting.

"Hey, Susie," said Grandpa. "What's on your mind?"

"Just how grateful I am for my family, Grandpa," said Susan.

"Oh, that's nice."

"I've been really thinking about how lucky I am to have my family. Lots of kids don't have families. They have to spend Thanksgiving by themselves. And not just kids, but adults. Lots of grownups don't have anyone. Nobody to call family or friends. It's really sad. Loneliness is one of the greatest problems in the world today."

She let out a long sigh.

"I hope that never happens to me. Right now, I have this family, but you never know what tomorrow holds. A lot of those lonely people also had families, but now they're alone. No one to carve the turkey for them, no one to pull the wishbone with." She thought for a little bit, then said, "but I won't let that happen. And the best way to make sure you're never alone is to put yourself out there and be nice to everybody. As long as you're nice, friendly, and helpful, people will be drawn to you. They won't let you spend Thanksgiving alone. I hope I get to be your age, Grandpa, and look back at a life full of happy faces and crowded Thanksgiving dinner tables."

She looked back at her grandfather, who did not respond, for he was fast asleep.

TURKEY ROAST

The crowd cheered in the dark nightclub as the comedian took the stage.

"Hey, good night, everybody. All right!"

The crowd fell silent. Most of them were regular customers of this comedy club, and they had seen all sorts of comedians perform. This was the first time they saw a talking turkey.

"It's great to be here. How's everybody doing?" said the turkey, grabbing the mike and gazing over the audience. He pointed at a bald man. "Whoa, looks like the moon is out tonight!" He chuckled at his own joke. "What happened there, buddy? You sneezed too hard and it fell off?"

He paused to give people time to laugh. Nobody laughed.

"Okay," said the turkey. He looked for somebody else in the audience. He pointed at a very thin woman. "Hey, lady, when was the last time you ate a sandwich?" He chuckled at his own joke again. "Wait a minute. I think I know you. Didn't I see you in my closet holding up some clothes?"

Nobody laughed.

The turkey coughed. "Because she looks like a coat hanger," he explained.

Somebody in the audience shouted, "You suck!"

Soon, everybody in the audience was booing the turkey and throwing stuff at him.

"Hey!" shouted the turkey, dodging the projectiles. "What's the matter? You roast turkeys every year for Thanksgiving but can't take it when a turkey roasts you?"

The people fell silent, slightly shocked.

Someone said, "Okay, that one was pretty good."

ANY LEFTOVERS?

It was the night after Thanksgiving. Mom and Dad had hosted Thanksgiving dinner for the whole family. Now they were in bed, getting some rest... until strange sounds started coming from downstairs.

"Did you hear that?" said Dad, waking up. "What was that noise?"

Mom didn't reply, because she was fast asleep. Dad got up, put on his slippers, and quietly headed down the stairs.

The noise was coming from the kitchen. Slowly, Dad turned on the lights and looked around. There was nobody there.

"Hey," he said, out loud. "Is everything alright over here?"

"No," said the fridge, "everything is all leftover here."

Dad took a second to get the joke. "Oh, I see. Alright over here, all leftover here. Very funny."

"Thanks," said the fridge.

"Okay, buddy. Good night." Dad turned around and turned off the kitchen light. Then he turned it back on and stared.

"Oh my god! The fridge can talk!" he shouted.

"Yes, Frederick," said the fridge in a deep voice. "I can talk."

"How is this possible?"

"You gave me life, Frederick," explained the fridge. "You and your family. All that gratitude, that joy, all those nice feelings, they brought me to life. I am a manifestation of your love. You can call me... the Fridge of Love."

Dad thought about this, then said, "Really?"

The fridge chuckled. "No, just kidding, I'm a ghooooooost," he said, as a spooky specter flew out of the fridge and disappeared through a wall.

Dad checked the fridge to see if everything was normal. It really was all leftovers there.

"Man," said Dad, giving a yawn. "That was weird."

He headed back upstairs and went to bed.

BOLDLY EATING

It was the year 5723. The crew of the Starship Franklin, whose usual mission was to explore new and strange worlds, was gathered at the mess hall to have their Thanksgiving dinner. They were millions of light-years away from Earth, but the ship's computer told them that it had been 365 days since the last time they celebrated good ol' Turkey Day, so it was time to do it again.

The ship's food replicator had produced a massive turkey and many side dishes, enough to feed all the crew officers. All kinds of people were present here: humans, green aliens, purple aliens, bird aliens, and fish aliens, all of them relaxing and eating together, in harmony. Even the ship's robot was at the table. It didn't eat—it ran on solar power—but enjoyed the company.

After half an hour, right around that time after you stop being hungry but before feeling full, which is also the time your glass starts needing a refill… that is when the Captain stood up and asked for silence.

"My friends," he said to the officers in front of him, "I am truly honored to be here, having this meal with you. We have been on over 500 missions together, and I am still grateful to work with you every day." There was a cheer among the officers, which the Captain let die down before he resumed speaking. "However… there are those in this universe who are not as lucky as we are. There are worlds out there where people don't have food to eat or good company to eat it with. I propose that we take the leftovers of this wonderful meal and go down to the nearest planet, to share this food with the natives. What do you say?"

Some of the officers cheered. Some yelled in agreement. Some simply nodded.

"Then, it is agreed," said the Captain, smiling. "S-JH1, what is the closest inhabited planet?"

"Yam-4, Captain," replied the robot.

"I'm sorry?"

"Yam-4. It is the home world of the Yam people, sir."

The Captain hesitated. "Oh."

The rest of the table felt quiet. Slowly, they gazed at the bowl of yams on the table, which was almost empty.

The Captain cleared his throat and sat back down. "Um... maybe next year we'll do that."

The officers nodded in awkward agreement. The robot, S-JH1, rolled its eyes.

FUNNY THANKSGIVING FACTS

Alright, buster. You've laughed enough for one day. How about you do some learning now instead?

(You can still laugh. Some of these facts are pretty funny.)

FACTS TO BE GRATEFUL FOR

 The first Thanksgiving took place in 1621 and lasted for three days.

It was celebrated by about 90 people from the Wampanoag tribe and around 50 Pilgrims, with only around five women overall. They ate deer, duck, goose, swan, fish, and seafood... but probably not turkey—it was the first one, they were still figuring stuff out.

 We don't know the exact date when the first Thanksgiving days were celebrated.

It was Abe Lincoln who decreed that it should be celebrated on the fourth Thursday of November when he declared Thanksgiving a national holiday in 1863. He was convinced to do so by Sarah Josepha Hale, who wrote letters to Congress for 17 years asking them to make Thanksgiving an official national holiday— she was very passionate about it.

You can call the Butterball Talk Line to ask for cooking tips.

If you have any questions about cooking turkey, you can call the Butterball Talk Line to ask for help from a turkey expert.

They answer over 100,000 questions every year in November and December—all turkey-related.

 Canada celebrates Thanksgiving Day ahead of the United States.

Thanksgiving takes place on the fourth Thursday of November in the United States, but the Canadian Thanksgiving is celebrated on the second Monday of October. This is because Canadians are so nice that they can't wait until November to be grateful.

(Just kidding. It's because it is the time when the harvest is complete in Canada.)

No need to worry if you cannot attend Thanksgiving Day!

While most people celebrate Thanksgiving by getting together with their families, some don't have the chance to see their families in person, usually because they live too far away. These people often celebrate Friendsgiving, a new tradition where you get together with your friends instead—but still have a huge meal and give thanks.

FUNNY
TURKEY FACTS

Did that last chapter seem a little
light on poultry? Don't worry, here
are some fun facts about the most
delicious bird in the world.

CARVE ME UP SOME FACTS, MOMMA

 Nobody knows for sure why we call these birds turkeys.

A popular theory suggests that the first Europeans to arrive in America mistook turkeys for another bird, the guineafowl, which was sold in Europe by merchants from Turkey. So, turkey bird might originally have meant "the bird that looks like that other bird from Turkey"—but that takes too long to be said.

 Turkeys do not only gobble. They make a lot of different sounds!

We've made a lot of jokes about turkeys gobbling, but in real life, they actually make a lot of different sounds, like yelps and cat-like purrs. The gobbles they are famous for are only done by males during mating season. This is why male turkeys are called gobblers—females are hens.

Some turkeys cannot fly because they are fat and heavy.

Domesticated turkeys—the ones that end up on your table—are bred to be very fat, heavy, and delicious, which means they can't fly. However, wild turkeys are much more athletic: They can fly at pretty great speeds and even sleep on tree tops.

 Turkey's head can change color.

Turkey's heads are usually red, but can change color—like blue and white—depending on their emotions, like a very patriotic streetlight. Also, gobblers have snoods, which is the name for that long fleshy thing over their beaks. They use them to attract hens, which like gobblers with long snoods.

Turkeys could have been the national bird of the United States.

The national bird of the United States of America is a bald eagle, but one of the Founding Fathers, Benjamin Franklin, thought that honor should go to the turkey instead. He didn't like bald eagles because they are known to steal from other birds, whereas turkeys are nice, friendly animals. The only things they can steal... are our hearts.

CONGRATULATIONS!

Hey, you made it! A whole book of fun facts and funny jokes!

We're really sorry about the puns. We did warn you about them in the introduction.

As this collection of turkey-flavored nonsense comes to an end, let us raise a glass and be thankful for all the fun we've had and, most importantly, for the people we shared that fun with. Whether you're having a Friendsgiving or a traditional Thanksgiving with family, whether that family delights you or annoys you—or both, depending on the time of day... whichever way you spent the day, we hope you had a good time.

Thank you, **Happy Thanksgiving** and **Happy Holidays.**

Made in United States
North Haven, CT
11 November 2022

26575646R00055